In th

His Crown

In the Interest of His Crown

Woman, you are seen by the King

Paula Joseph

Cover design and image by Dusty and Kirsten Voorhees (ReJoyed.com)

Edited and page layout, and graphic design by Dusty Voorhees

Cover image provided by Canva

Scripture quotations are taken from the 'Holy Bible,' King James Version.

CONTENTS

Preface

A while back I received a package in the mail. When I opened it I found a beautiful note from my friend Paula that said something like "I sent this, but it is from God to remind you that you are a daughter of the King." It was a crown. That crown now sits in a prominent place in my home to remind me of who I am in Christ and how I am seen by my Heavenly Father, the King of Kings.

Psalm 103:1-5 says it so beautifully:

1 Bless the LORD, O my soul: and all that is within me, bless his holy name.

2 Bless the LORD, O my soul, and forget not all his benefits:

3 Who forgiveth all thine iniquities; who healeth all thy diseases;

4 Who redeemeth thy life from destruction; who crowneth thee with lovingkindness and tender mercies;

5 Who satisfieth thy mouth with good things; so that thy youth is renewed like the eagle's.

You see, I haven't always been a princess, and there are still moments I don't act like one. I've needed redemption from destruction; we all do.

The author of Psalm 103 is preaching to his own soul. First reminding himself who God is (holy) and what he does (benefits, forgives, redeems) and then gives us a CROWN of loving kindness and tender mercies!   God literally takes us from the pit to the palace. Woman, if that is not Good News, I don't know what is.

God wants to meet you in your destruction, your despair, your abandonment, your hopelessness, your vulnerability, your sin, and give you a crown.   Don't believe it? Read on sister!   You are about to meet some very special women, including my dear friend Paula, that are seen, known, and loved by the King of Kings.

Kirsten Voorhees

HATH GOD SAID

Before the fall of man, the King of Kings had long been in the courts of the kingdom with His Father, God, and the Holy Spirit.

Before creation, God was. There has never been a time when He was not.

Before creation, Jesus was. There has never been a time when He was not.

Before creation, the Holy Spirit was. There has never been a time when the Spirit was not.

Before I can begin to tell you how much the Father loves the woman you are, I must take you back to that moment in the garden where the Woman was deceived. Her deception has long been our shame, shame we have been raised in, shame that would lead many of us to believe that God does not love women as much as men. Simply put, we believe on some subconscious level we are not good enough. The truth is… that is a lie. A lie the devil would love to see you bound by.

God showed me something so profound and continues to share His heart with me through scripture. It is my prayer that you hear God's heart. God has a heart, and you are in it!

You are a beautiful woman.

- A woman designed after God's own heart
- A woman fashioned in your mother's womb
- A woman God called by name
- A woman God knew from the foundation of the earth

You are that woman; the woman God is in love with and to prove it I must take you back to the beginning of the Word.

Before the fall, Adam had a beautiful relationship with God.

God's heart was tender toward the man he created, so tender was his love that he looked upon Adam and said, "It is not good that the man should be alone." This moved God into another creative position, a position of love, loyalty, and compassion. God longed to give Adam the gift of companionship. God could relate to us then and He can relate to us now, but like Adam, we do not always know how to relate to God. He is God after all!

While Adam was in a deep sleep, God removed one of Adam's ribs to create the woman and not just any woman — a gift. God was eager to present his gift to his friend, Adam. God wanted Adam to experience every aspect of paradise in the garden of Eden. Keep in mind that God touched Adam to remove his rib to create you.

Everything else God created, He did by using words, "Let there be…" The word 'Let' means to overcome an obstacle, it also means do not prevent, but allow. The Bible says, "If any man have an ear, let him hear," that being something Jesus said many times in the new testament. Again, let means 'to allow.'

> *Let this mind be in you, which was also in Christ Jesus: who, being in the form of God, thought it not robbery to be equal with God: but made himself of no reputation, and took on the form of a servant, and was made in the likeness of men: and being found in fashion as a man, he*

humbled himself, and became obedient unto death, even the death of the cross. Philippians 2:5-8

Many believe that the word 'let' means 'listen' whereas it means 'allow'. 'Let' was and is part of God's creative dialect when he speaks life into or over anything. This phrase then must overcome the obstacle that is in the way, such as our flesh, dull hearing, or our unwillingness to hear God on any level much less a natural one. Why? Because until we really get to know God, his voice is foreign to our natural nature. Adam and the Woman, however, not only walked with God, but they also talked with God.

The Bible says that God created Adam from the dust/clay of the earth. God could have spoken the woman into creation just as He did with Adam. Instead, He touched Adam to create the woman, how profound is that! This is also the moment where he becomes the great physician... technically speaking... God removed Adam's rib after he put him in a deep sleep to create you and yet Adam felt no pain.

Can you image how pleased God must've been to give Adam a companion? Although they were not married by the law of Moses this couple was indeed one flesh.

God then walked with both Adam and the Woman in the cool of the day.

They had conversations with God.

They had fellowship with God.

Wild was the love of God for them both, male and female.

Let me point out that just because every conversation God had with them is not recorded, scripturally does not make this point moot.

That means that when the woman in Genesis Chapter 3 has an encounter with the serpent everything she said was true of God; she knew God and she knew what God told her, making her answer truthfully. It is often preached that Eve was deceived and added to the word, but it is "the woman" who was deceived, as her name was not yet Eve, and she did not add to the word of God.

The woman was not deceptive in nature until she defied God by doing what God warned her not to do. God warned them then and God warns us today. God is our Father, and a good Father tells his children to take heed to those things that are dangerous to us. Should our Heavenly Father be different than a natural man who knows extraordinarily little compared to the all-knowing eternal Godhead that knows all things.

 I am not here to point out her sin alone, but to shine light on that moment in the garden, a moment I have never heard preached. So, by God's grace and with the help of the Holy Spirit and the Word of God I am going to point out something profoundly significant.

Remember, the woman also walked with God.

Keep in mind she had no ill will in her heart.

She did not know the difference between good and evil.

She could not add to the word, to do so would be deceptive and suggest that God's plan for the woman was marred with a mistake and the moment we teach from the pulpit that the woman added to the word of God; we then add to the word a belief that is not supported anywhere scripturally.

The woman was duped by a greater lie that began with a question... "Hath God said?". To this day we struggle with that question. The enemy picks on us the same way he did in the beginning and sadly, sometimes we fall for the lie.

- ♚ It may be the lie that we are not good enough
- ♚ That we are not saved by grace
- ♚ That we are fake, false, and foolish to believe that God is for us and not against us.

The serpent began with a question. When you are hit with the question answer the liar with the truth, and that truth can only come from the word of God. Trust me, the more you know about your loving Father, the creator, the more you know about yourself, and the more you know about the devil.

When the serpent came to beguile the woman, he began planting seeds of doubt. He wanted her to explore all the options and let's say this... just because you can explore all the worldly options it does not mean you should. We have free will.

Unlike us, the Woman did not know how to lie.

The Woman's eyes had not been opened to sin. Everything she knew up to that point was pure, honest, lovely, and had a good report. After all, she was in paradise with a very real and living God, a God who created her in love.

The Woman loved God, so when she responds to the serpent that came to beguile her, she not only speaks the truth, but the Woman does it out of a pure heart.

Watch this...

It truly gets deep...

...Pay attention this is a free from shame moment and the first sin truly committed; a sin that would go on to open the woman's eyes. The first sin recorded in the bible was not the moment the woman ate the fruit... read this and see it for yourself.

Genesis Chapter 3

¹ Now the serpent was more subtil than any beast of the field which the LORD God had made. And he said unto the woman, Yea, hath God said, Ye shall not eat of every tree of the garden?

² And the woman said unto the serpent, We may eat of the fruit of the trees of the garden: ³ But of the fruit of the tree which is in the midst of the garden, God hath said, ...

Keep in mind the Woman had never sinned against God and she certainly could not articulate a lie much less conceive one... In other words when she goes on to answer the serpent, she tells him all that God had said. I know I sound redundant, but I want to drive home the truth...

'Hath God said,'

The woman answered,

> ^{3} ... *Ye shall not eat of it, neither shall ye touch it, lest ye die.*

This was a true statement. The Serpent then goes on to lie to the woman.

> ^{4} *And the serpent said unto the woman, Ye shall not surely die.*

Here is the truth about that text... not only did God say do not eat of the tree, He also told the woman do not to touch it.

This then became the first act of disobedience, the moment she touched the fruit. (Notice I said fruit and not an apple). The first sin committed, according to the text, was the moment the woman ate the fruit. Furthermore, you cannot eat something without touching it. Disobedient or not, she would have never known the grave consequences that God warned her about had she not touched and eaten the fruit.

What has God warned you not to do?

Things we desire cannot kill us if we do not touch them.

Be mindful of the things you touch!

It is equally important to note that the spiritual laws and rules of paradise were, and have always been, in effect and did not affect the woman until she ate the fruit. The consequence of that act of disobedience has left us marred with a perpetual state of knowing good and evil... something we would not know if the woman did not touch it to begin with.

Crack, Heroine, Crystal Meth, Alcohol and Cigarettes cannot kill you if you do not touch them.

I could preach a sermon on that alone, but I want to point out how much God adores you.

God told the Woman not to touch it, not to eat it; He did this out of love.

 The dialog continues well after their eyes were opened, God cried out to them and ask,

> *11 Who told thee thou was naked? Hast thou eaten of the tree, whereof I commanded thee that thou shouldest not eat?*
>
> *12 And the man said, 'The woman whom thou gavest to be with me, she gave me of the tree, and I did eat.*

Notice Adam uses a transitional word that lines up with all that the woman told the serpent, all while blaming God with the same word, "Gavest me" and "she gave me" ...

To expound on the word "gave," Adam had to touch the fruit in order to eat it. Remember, God had to touch Adam to create the Woman. First, Adam blames God, then the Woman. If you read more of the text you will see that God already had a plan and that plan was Jesus and Jesus had a crown...

> *Genesis 3:15 And I will put enmity between thee and the woman, and between thy seed and her seed; it shall bruise thy head, and thou shalt bruise his heel.*

- ♔ God had no choice but to put things in order...
- ♔ The rules of paradise had been broken
- ♔ God did not yell at her, scream at her, or blame her. Instead, He does something beautiful most never see...

Please, keep in mind I am not saying the Woman was not deceived, she was!

But God... God promises to use the very vessel (a woman) that was deceived to deceive the deceiver, and it worked. Glory to God (See 1 Corinthians 2:4-8).

All of that and yet God did not name the woman 'Eve,' Adam did.

God's plan not only involved redemption but an inheritance, an invitation to the kingdom. Most people never realize how hard it was for the very God of love to pass down a death sentence upon His only son Jesus. Genesis 3:15 and John 3:16 reveal God's plan that we might be redeemed.

This is love!!! ...Woman, you are loved.

- ♔ God knows you.
- ♔ God knows who you are.
- ♔ God knows what you have done.

- ♚ God knows you were hurt, beaten, abused, tricked, and yes, deceived
- ♚ ... But God has a heart for you and His big is bigger than your big
- ♚ God wants to redeem.
- ♚ Restore

And Crown you with His love

God wants to give you...

- ♚ Beauty for ashes
- ♚ The oil of joy for mourning
- ♚ The garment of praise for the spirit of heaviness

...God wants to share His heart with you

"But you don't know me."

"No, but I know myself and I know God."

I lived in darkness, tasted darkness unlike any darkness I had ever known.

Sin does not look any different on you than it does on me...

Sin is deceptive.

But isn't that the point?

... and yet, God knows us and loves us, despite us.

The law of sin is in our nature, our DNA, until we confess our sins and declare that Jesus is Lord.

Jesus freed us from the law of sin and death that was set in motion way back at the beginning of time...

But what does sin look like?

> *"Now the works of the flesh are manifest, which are these; adultery, fornication, uncleanness, lasciviousness, idolatry, witchcraft, hatred, variance, emulations, wrath, strife, seditions, heresies, envyings, murders, drunkenness, revellings, and such like..." Galatians 5:19 - 21a*

In other words, we cannot blame these things on the devil

> *"For from within, out of the heart of men, proceed evil thoughts, adulteries, fornications, murders, thefts, covetousness, wickedness, deceit, lasciviousness, an evil eye, blasphemy, pride, foolishness: All these evil things come from within, and defile the man." Mark 7: 21*

> *"If we say that we have no sin, we deceive ourselves, and the truth is not in us." 1 John 1:8*

> *"For all have sinned, and come short of the glory of God;" Romans 3:23*

There is not one person on earth that has not committed sin. The Bible says there is none righteous, no not one.

The beauty of God's love is that He already knows the nature of your sin, and that by the law you were bound to it, until Jesus died on the cross for you.

"For he hath made him to be sin for us, who knew no sin; that we might be made the righteousness of God in him." 2 Corinthians 5:21 KJV

Jesus's DNA was pure and sin free until He became what he was not so that we could become what we never have been...

- ♙ ...made right with God
- ♙ Now, Daddy's door is open.
- ♙ God wants to talk to you.

The word of God tells us,

> *"Let us therefore come boldly unto the throne of grace, that we may obtain mercy, and find grace to help in time of need." Hebrews 4:16 KJV*

> *Removing the obstacle that once separated us from him, thereby allowing us to come boldly without hesitation, fear, or trembling. 'Let'*

God gives us the confidence we need to approach His throne room, day or night.

- ♙ God never slumbers.
- ♙ He never sleeps.

God's hand is not shortened that it cannot save, neither is his ear heavy that He cannot hear.

- ♙ He hears you.
- ♙ God's eyes are set upon you.
- ♙ He adores you.

God said, "though your sins be like scarlet I will wash them white as snow..."

For the record, the Bible says, "God is not a man that He should lie."

We have all been lied too, but God cannot defy the embodiment of who He is… any more than He could go against what He said.

He is a covenant keeping God.

Our Heavenly Father keeps His promises…

- ♚ Even if your sin is ever before you
- ♚ Even if you have done too much
- ♚ Even if you walked away from God, one too many times
- ♚ Even if you got dirty on your way home

God sees you through the eyes of his only begotten son, Jesus, even if you do not.

The truth is because of Jesus you have been acquitted of ALL wrongdoing…

Jesus is seated at the right hand of God, he lives to make intercession on your behalf (Praise God, Jesus is praying for you!).

Jesus is not finished with you; besides, you are His Bride and what a beautiful Bride you are!

You see your dirt…

…He sees your gown

You see your past mistakes…

…He sees your crown

Perception and reality are two different things, for example: because of the law of gravity, we are upside down in the center of the universe, just because we do not perceive it, it does not make it any less true.

In other words, just because you do not feel forgiven it does not mean that you have not been forgiven.

Trust God with your feelings, do not trust yourself with them...

After all, how has that worked out for you?

Let's go on a journey together and glance at the lives of some women in the Bible who were a 'written off mess'...

- ♛ Yes, God uses messed up situations.
- ♛ God loved them in their mess...
- ♛ Right where they were...
- ♛ Just as He loves you in your mess.

I pray that as you look at these women God will reveal His love to you through the power of the Holy Spirit.

Hagar and Sarai

What they were, or what they did was not as important as who they became...

Genesis 16

> *¹ Now Sarai Abram's wife bare him no children: and she had an handmaid, an Egyptian, whose name was Hagar.*
>
> *² And Sarai said unto Abram, Behold now, the LORD hath restrained me from bearing: I pray thee, go in unto my maid; it may be that I may obtain children by her. And Abram hearkened to the voice of Sarai.*
>
> *³ And Sarai Abram's wife took Hagar her maid the Egyptian, after Abram had dwelt ten years in the land of Canaan, and gave her to her husband Abram to be his wife.*

This is where trouble begins in the family...

> *⁴ And he went in unto Hagar, and she conceived: and when she saw that she had conceived, her mistress was despised in her eyes. ⁵ And Sarai said unto Abram, My wrong be upon thee: I have given my maid into thy bosom; and when she saw that she had conceived, I was despised in her eyes: the LORD judge between me and thee.*

Sarai/Sarah... Blames Abram/Abraham for the trouble brewing even though it was her idea to begin with by bringing Hagar into their marriage bed as a surrogate. Not only does she blame him; she wants God to judge the matter.

On some level, Sarai must have believed she was doing a good thing.

But doing a good thing does not make it a God thing...

Have you ever gotten ahead of God's plan?

Have you brought your good idea in to your own relationship or household only to be troubled by the consequences of the decision?

I am guilty, but I thank God that He can use those situations and set us before kings, and not just kings, but nations.

> *6 But Abram said unto Sarai, Behold, thy maid is in thy hand; do to her as it pleaseth thee. And when Sarai dealt hardly with her, she fled from her face*

Wait, I feel empathy for Hagar. After all she was only doing that which was asked of her. Hagar was a servant, one that could not deal with how Sarai began to treat her. As a result, Hagar flees into the wilderness, and the angel of the Lord found her by a fountain of water; then the angel addresses her not only by name but

- ♚ By her position
- ♚ Her rank
- ♚ Her status

> *7 And the angel of the LORD found her by a fountain of water in the wilderness, by the fountain in the way to Shur. 8 And he said, Hagar, Sarai's maid, whence camest thou? and whither wilt thou go? And she said, I flee from*

> the face of my mistress Sarai. *⁹ And the angel of the LORD said unto her, Return to thy mistress, and submit thyself under her hands. ¹⁰ And the angel of the LORD said unto her, I will multiply thy seed exceedingly, that it shall not be numbered for multitude.*

Sometimes God will begin the conversation. Hagar did not have to utter a word...

"While you are yet speaking, I will answer thee", that is a promise God made.

Your wilderness experience just might be your refuge, a time set apart to encounter a very real and living God, despite your reason for being there...

Hagar was silent but keep in mind the angel of the Lord already knew why she fled. The angel was familiar with her affliction and yet the angel talked with her and told to return and submit.

Now, that is a job I would want to quit...

... but Hagar went back, and she went back with a blessing spoken over her life, and a private encounter that would someday change her life.

> *¹¹ And the angel of the LORD said unto her, Behold, thou art with child, and shalt bear a son, and shalt call his name Ishmael; because the LORD hath heard thy affliction*

I love this part!

... "Because the Lord hath heard thy affliction."

    ♟ Wow, the Lord heard her affliction.

    ♟ When God hears our heart, He shows up.

12 And he will be a wild man; his hand will be against every man, and every man's hand against him; and he shall dwell in the presence of all his brethren. 13 And she called the name of the LORD that spake unto her, Thou God seest me: for she said, Have I also here looked after him that seeth me?

In verse 13 Hagar goes on to say, *"thou God seest me,"*

Hagar names the well Beerlahairoi, which means, *the well of him that liveth and seeth me* Or *the well of the vision of life.*

So deep! God heard the affliction of a servant girl, and I love this, not only did He hear her affliction, He promised to set her son up with a life that a handmaid could only dream of, and that promise would bring freedom to Hagar...

Hagar had what I would call an encounter with God.

    God saw her...

        God sees you.

Even if, like Sarai, you started the mess, remember, God is in the details. Yes, God is in all the messy details. I hope you find time to read those chapters in Genesis. Right now, I am going to skip to the next encounter Hagar has...

Genesis 21

> ⁵ *And Abraham was an hundred years old, when his son Isaac was born unto him.*
>
> ⁶ *And Sarah said, God hath made me to laugh, so that all that hear will laugh with me.*
>
> ⁷ *And she said, Who would have said unto Abraham, that Sarah should have given children suck? for I have born him a son in his old age.*
>
> ⁸ *And the child grew, and was weaned: and Abraham made a great feast the same day that Isaac was weaned.*

The promised seed both Sarah and Abraham had been waiting for has been born, named, and weaned, but a problem arises from what seems like out of nowhere...

I call this problem jealousy, one of the many works of our flesh, and Sarah struggled with it too.

> ⁹ *And Sarah saw the son of Hagar the Egyptian, which she had born unto Abraham, mocking.*
>
> ¹⁰ *Wherefore she said unto Abraham, Cast out this bondwoman and her son: for the son of this bondwoman shall not be heir with my son, even with Isaac.*

When we first learn of Hagar she is referred to as Sarai's handmaid, then she is called her servant, later in the story she is called the bondwoman... it is as if she is being demoted every time Sarah lays eyes on her.

And yet, Abraham is grieved but God tells Abraham to do all that Sarah has asked

God says

> *¹³ And also of the son of the bondwoman will I make a nation, because he is thy seed. ¹⁴ And Abraham rose up early in the morning, and took bread, and a bottle of water, and gave it unto Hagar, putting it on her shoulder, and the child, and sent her away: and she departed, and wandered in the wilderness of Beersheba.*

It might seem like Abraham has no feelings, but it is the way he gives Hagar (not the bondwoman) water. Rather than handing it to her, Abraham shows compassion by putting it on her shoulder and does the same with his son.

Keep in Mind: she is not going to the same wilderness she ran to years earlier when she encountered the angel of the Lord.

> *¹⁵ And the water was spent in the bottle, and she cast the child under one of the shrubs.*

> *¹⁶ And she went, and sat her down over against him a good way off, as it were a bowshot: for she said, Let me not see the death of the child. And she sat over against him, and lift up her voice, and wept.*

This is where I wonder, why is she crying? She did not cry when she made the decision to leave the first time, so why now?... where was her confidence?... what happened to her faith? After all she said, *"the well of him that liveth and seeth me."*

It is almost poetic, and sad. Surely, she must have felt the years of tension building, boiling over, and at the very least, she must have seen this day coming, but the truth is she did not see it coming.

Why? Because she knew what the Lord said to her; she believed the first report. On the other hand, she failed to realize this was not going to happen in Sarai's dwelling. Hagar must have thought all along that her cruel mistress would see her son grow into a man of promise, and because of that, Hagar, like most women, got comfortable, even when things were uncomfortable.

But the One that did see this moment coming was truly the only One that mattered.

God saw Hagar.

I can relate to Hagar. By now she is known by so many different titles, only to find that entitlement of a first-born son brought no entitlement at all, or does God see it differently? Remember, Sarah was worried Ishmael would be an heir. Sarah failed to realize that God had a plan for Ishmael.

Say this out loud, "God has a plan!"

Watch this...

We tend to forget that

- ♟ God fixes
- ♟ God restores
- ♟ God provides
- ♟ God listens
- ♟ God speaks

...and yet there are days, messed up days, that I forget to look at what the Lord has done for me. I forget *to lift up mine eyes unto the hills, from whence cometh my help* (Psalm 121:1), in other words, I am no different than Hagar.

...Can you relate?

I love this...

> *17a And God heard the voice of the lad; and the angel of God called to Hagar out of heaven, and said unto her, What aileth thee, Hagar?*

Wait, this is the desire of every woman, that God would hear her child. What a beautiful blessing.

Keep in mind the angel of the Lord does not address her as Sarah's handmaid this time, and rather than ask her, whence camest thou, and whither where thou go? Instead, the angel says 'fear not'

17b fear not; for God hath heard the voice of the lad where he is.

18 Arise, lift up the lad, and hold him in thine hand; for I will make him a great nation.

19 And God opened her eyes, and she saw a well of water; and she went, and filled the bottle with water, and gave the lad drink.

20 And God was with the lad; and he grew, and dwelt in the wilderness, and became an archer.

21 And he dwelt in the wilderness of Paran: and his mother took him a wife out of the land of Egypt.

Here is another deep thought: Hagar was the first servant mentioned in the Bible to suffer under harsh punishment.

Even deeper, take note, the first time in the wilderness

God heard her affliction.

She acknowledged, 'God sees me.'

The second time in the wilderness which would have been like a death sentence

- Hagar's son was heard
- God hears me and God hears you

God fulfilled all the promises He made to Hagar, to make her descendants so numerous that they were too many to count.

Even if Sarah could care less, God cared.

I am not saying Sarah was evil, she was desperate, then jealous...

Mix desperation with jealousy and you will have a devastating outcome. Believe me,

-God saw Hagar's affliction...

♔ He sees your affliction.
♔ God heard Hagar, and He hears you...

God is yet again moved with compassion, this time on behalf of Hagar. God created a well where there was not a well, this being a foreshadow of the woman Jesus would go on to encounter at Jacob's well. Isn't that ironic?

Lastly, when the angel of the Lord appeared to Hagar and spoke her name, he did it without any affiliation to Sarah... it seems what the angel of the Lord was really saying was, 'you are free'.

The other thing to keep in mind is that when Hagar ran the first time, she was a slave, bought and paid for out of Egypt. Leaving could have cost Hagar her life, just as returning could have been at the expense of severe and cruel punishment.

All of this and yet God had a plan for

♔ the handmaid
♔ the servant
♔ the bondmaid
♔ Hagar

God set Hagar, the woman, free.

Hagar was no longer bound to anyone other than God.

Rahab the Harlot

In the book of Joshua, we meet Rahab the Harlot. Look at the lengths God went to for *the woman* he created.

Rahab was known for being a harlot, you could not have a reputation worse than that of a prostitute, …

but she was in survival mode, …

and no woman knows the length she will go to in order to survive, but God does!

The Bible doesn't indicate why she chose the profession of a harlot, but what she does is incredible. Her actions were so incredible that she is not only mentioned in the Old Testament, but also noted in the New Testament as well. Rahab is the only woman mentioned in what we call the hall of fame/faith found in the books of Hebrews, Matthew, and James.

Follow me here, I know why I chose to dance

- ♛ I admit I loved dancing
- ♛ I loved the strobe lights
- ♛ I loved the darkness
- ♛ I loved the euphoric feeling of control

I, like Rahab, know what it is like to have a reputation of ill repute

- ♛ I brought shame to the family name
- ♛ I lived recklessly
- ♛ I believed I was not good enough
- ♛ I believed I deserved my reputation, over my heart

But God...

God is a God who removes guilt...

Removes shame...

and sets you up for an encounter with Him...

and that is exactly what He does for Rahab the Harlot.

Joshua 2

> *[1] And Joshua the son of Nun sent out of Shittim two men to spy secretly, saying, Go view the land, even Jericho. And they went, and came into an harlot's house, named Rahab, and lodged there.*
>
> *[2] And it was told the king of Jericho, saying, Behold, there came men in hither to night of the children of Israel to search out the country.*
>
> *[3] And the king of Jericho sent unto Rahab, saying, Bring forth the men that are come to thee, which are entered into thine house: for they be come to search out all the country.*

Since the king, was aware of the strangers entering into Jericho, the city was closed to traffic and on high alert because the kingdom had been infiltrated by men that sought to destroy them...

God used a prostitute, a harlot, a woman with not only a reputation, but a bad one at that.

Perhaps Rahab's dwelling place was upon entering the gates of a town.

But if Rahab were a "strangers" first encounter, why would they trust her? That is the equivalent of walking in a red-light district today and getting robbed, or worse, killed. If these two men of God had been caught that is exactly what would have happened, they would have been killed.

> [4] *And the woman took the two men, and hid them, and said thus, There came men unto me, but I wist not whence they were:*

Rahab told a lie that could have gotten her killed when she said she did not know where they had come from.

"And the woman," notice in this text, she is not called the harlot, instead she is called the woman. That is the same state of the woman who would become known as Eve after Adam renamed her.

> [5] *And it came to pass about the time of shutting of the gate, when it was dark, that the men went out: whither the men went I wot not: pursue after them quickly; for ye shall overtake them.*

In other words, Rahab's second lie was that she did not know which way they went.

> [6] *But she had brought them up to the roof of the house, and hid them with the stalks of flax, which she had laid in order upon the roof.*

> *[7] And the men pursued after them the way to Jordan unto the fords: and as soon as they which pursued after them were gone out, they shut the gate.*

At this point, it is no one in/no one out. Rahab is not only in a compromising position, but she is also in a life-threatening position. On both sides at that, had she been caught, her king could have had her killed...

> ...and the two men who went to spy out the land could have killed her, a no-win situation

> > but God had a plan to use her despite her reputation.

In the Old Testament, Rahab would have been shunned by everyone, including her family, for living her life outside of their moral standard. She was unethical. She also had no right to marry, or to be given in marriage. How could she be a hero with a life of disgrace towering above her. Rahab was known by both men and her family, and their report would not be a good one

Her reputation preceded her... they were so caught up with what she did...

> ... that they could not see who she could become.

When no one sees you...

The real you...

It stings...

... And it stings when people you love bask in the 'You should have done this, that, or the other with your life, look at yourself.'

I can say that because I have heard those words

.... And I thought, 'Why can't you see my heart?'

While Rahab might have felt dismissed, overlooked, and forsaken, she seized the opportunity to get to know the God of Israel, the very God who would not only forgive her, but would remember her sin no more.

Instead, God remembers the one thing she did on behalf of His name.

Rahab was wise enough to know a death sentence loomed over the land. What did she have to lose? Her life at that point was already over, but watch what happens in these scriptures

8 And before they were laid down, she came up unto them upon the roof;

9 And she said unto the men, I know that the LORD hath given you the land, and that your terror is fallen upon us, and that all the inhabitants of the land faint because of you.

[10]For we have heard how the LORD dried up the water of the Red sea for you, when ye came out of Egypt; and what ye did unto the two kings of the Amorites, that were on the other side Jordan, Sihon and Og, whom ye utterly destroyed.

[11]And as soon as we had heard these things, our hearts did melt, neither did there remain any more courage in any man, because of you: for the LORD your God, he is God in heaven above, and in earth beneath.

Rahab the Harlot knew four things

- ♟ The Lord has given them the land
- ♟ Terror has fallen upon her people
- ♟ The Canaanites faint because of them
- ♟ More importantly, she knew, The LORD their God, He was and is God in heaven above and in the earth beneath.

Yes, a harlot

A prostitute

...Knew the God of Israel, so much so, that Rahab begged the spies

[12]Now therefore, I pray you, swear unto me by the LORD, since I have shewed you kindness, that ye will also shew kindness unto my father's house, and give me a true token:

[13]And that ye will save alive my father, and my mother, and my brethren, and my sisters, and all that they have, and deliver our lives from death.

Can you image how courageous the harlot had to be? She certainly had tenacity, after all, she bargained with the men of God

Rahab was bold enough to seek safety for herself and the safety of her family and all that belonged to them.

Sometimes in life you find yourself loving people who may not necessarily know how to show you love...

...but love them anyway

> *14 And the men answered her, Our life for yours, if ye utter not this our business. And it shall be, when the LORD hath given us the land, that we will deal kindly and truly with thee.*
>
> *15 Then she let them down by a cord through the window: for her house was upon the town wall, and she dwelt upon the wall.*

Talk about having a bird's eye view, Rahab could see all those coming and going, no wonder the king sent word to her.

Furthermore, little does Rahab know the very cord she used to let them down would be the same cord used to save her life and her family.

Think about this, I was a dancer in a gentleman's club and as bad as that might come across; it is because of my so-called occupation that I had an encounter with God. God took the mess I made with my life and drew me out of darkness that I might have true fellowship with the light. I, like Rahab, knew about God, heard of Him, learned of Him, but I did not have a genuine encounter with God until he brought Godly women into the club. When the other dancers teased me, I said, "While you are joking God might be trying to get our attention."

At that point in my life God sent Godly women to get my attention...

...Just as God sent two spies to get Rahab's attention. That means that what we do after He has gotten our attention matters.

Look at this...

> *16 And she said unto them, Get you to the mountain, lest the pursuers meet you; and hide yourselves there three days, until the pursuers be returned: and afterward may ye go your way.*

Hold on, what could a prostitute offer and why would the spies take her word for it? Simply put they knew if anyone knew the city, she did. At this point both the spies and Rahab have to rely on each other merely by their word.

> *17 And the men said unto her, We will be blameless of this thine oath which thou hast made us swear.*

> *18 Behold, when we come into the land, thou shalt bind this line of scarlet thread in the window which thou didst let us down by: and thou shalt bring thy father, and thy mother, and thy brethren, and all thy father's household, home unto thee.*

> [19] *And it shall be, that whosoever shall go out of the doors of thy house into the street, his blood shall be upon his head, and we will be guiltless: and whosoever shall be with thee in the house, his blood shall be on our head, if any hand be upon him.*

Side note, check this out, it is not a coincidence. The cord mentioned earlier was just a cord to aid those coming and going. However, this cord would be referred to as a scarlet cord, an implication of hope and symbolic of the blood applied to the doors of the Israelites when they were told to apply blood with a hyssop branch and stay inside. Furthermore, anyone who did not do as they were told would lose their first-born child. The same was true of Rahab and her family; had any one in her household disobeyed, they would have been killed

> [20] *And if thou utter this our business, then we will be quit of thine oath which thou hast made us to swear.*

Rahab was known for many things, and yet, many people fail to realize how smart she was. Imagine a prostitute going home to her natural father, mother, and brother, only to beg them to trust her, come home with her, and abide with her...

> ... in a house that probably reeked with her distasteful lifestyle.

But, Rahab made a contractual agreement with the spies. Despite her occupation, she knew God was big enough to not only save her, but all who were dear to her, and her plan worked.

Rahab had to commit treason against her natural king to serve the only King that mattered — God.

- ♕ She lied to the king
- ♕ She covered up the spies
- ♕ She gave them directions

All while making them swear an oath; an oath the LORD would not break because He is a covenant keeping GOD

Rahab was probably a woman in her 20's or 30's who'd grown up hearing about God's might and terrifying works. God parted the Red Sea 40 years before this encounter, well into her past. Who knows how old she was, but because she heard of God, she was bold. Her faith saved her entire family.

- ♕ We have all lied
- ♕ We have all covered things up
- ♕ We have all kept secrets

By the way, that is what the spies were referring to when they told Rahab not once but twice, *"If ye utter not this our business"*

Joshua 6:25

> *25 And Joshua saved Rahab the harlot alive, and her father's household, and all that she had; and she dwelleth in Israel even unto this day; because she hid the messengers, which Joshua sent to spy out Jericho.*

Rahab is remarkable in that she saw destruction coming and gave up her lifestyle of sin that she might dwell among the Israelites.

Here is another interesting fact in Joshua 2:23, 24 we see the report of the two spies. Note the two spies use not only Rahab's report but her words, 'For even all the inhabitants of the country do faint because of us.' (Joshua 2:9) Keep in mind they did not encounter anyone other than Rahab who had firsthand knowledge of her land's terrors.

I love how God chose to use a woman to tell a story. Rahab did not embellish she told the spies the truth and because of her firsthand knowledge of how mighty God is and was she placed her fate in His hands the moment she hid the two spies

I noticed something so beautiful...

- ♚ Most of the women God encountered were alone, and not just alone, but lived hard lives...
- ♚ And not for nothing it is when I am alone that I can hear God
- ♚ Or cry out to God and spend time dwelling in the presence of God

Rahab secured her future and was an ancestor of King David. It is through David's line that Jesus, the Messiah, was born.

...But God moves outside of the norm and creates room for a messed-up woman like Rahab where most people would not...

Rahab was part of God's plan all along, He used her in the 'Big Plan' called salvation. Can you imagine having a prostitute in your lineage?

- ♟ I rejoice in that because if God can use a harlot, He can use me...
- ♟ He can use you...
- ♟ He can step into your mess and give you advice

So often we are caught up in things we don't know how to change...

> Even when we know that on the other side of the decision is destruction!

- ♟ We feel trapped
- ♟ We want to do right
- ♟ We want to walk away from that toxic relationship

The truth is, apart from Christ Jesus, we can do nothing.

I knew while writing this book that God was going to show me a pattern to His love.

- ♟ God is merciful with the woman in the garden of Eden
- ♟ God saw Hagar
- ♟ God heard Hagar's son
- ♟ And God saved Rahab the harlot and her family

God cannot separate himself from the Word, anymore than we can separate ourselves from our soul. It is in us; it makes us who we are. I feel sorrow in my spirit when I think about God's love in the Old Testament and how few ever get to see it because we have learned to read the Word of God with a spirit of condemnation and legalism.

From three different stories we can see a pattern of God's unfailing love. He meets each woman's need regardless of how bleak it appeared, and He made something beautiful out of their lives.

God will meet you in your mess.

God will meet you in your wilderness.

God will meet you in your city.

Let God walk into your poor decisions, your occupation, your wilderness!

Your life will not look the same, it cannot, because wherever God is… the outcome changes. While God is changing the outcome, He is also changing you, perfecting you, and then presenting you as a trophy of His grace.

These women were not quitters…

Even when Hagar wanted to give up, the angels of the Lord told her go back and submit.

In fact, in Rahab's case one could argue she was persistent.

All that to say no matter what you are going through do not quit

Be bold

And persistent

The Daughters Mentioned in Proverbs 31
Turn to Proverbs Chapter 31 (a picture of virtue)

I am relatively certain you can find a book about the Proverbs 31 woman; I want to point out one scripture most often neglected and reveal to you the character traits of the woman:

> *[29] Many daughters have done virtuously, but thou excellest them all.*

Whereas the Proverbs 31 woman was all these things:

- Morally upright in her heart
- Intelligent
- Invaluable, she considered a field before she bought it
- She was always busy
- Considerate
- Kind
- Cautious
- Skillful
- Wise
- Fearless
- Yet fears God…
  … A healthy, reverential fear
- She was and is inspirational
- She was strong
- She looked after her family
- And she also looked after the poor
- Her works praised her in the city gates

… And yet,

> *29 Many daughters have done virtuously, but thou*
> *excellest them all.*

How come we do not talk about these daughters?

The truth is we see what we have been taught to see

I believe God is moving us into a dispensation in time where we are going to have to go to the word of God and search the scriptures for ourselves…

Seek ye first the Kingdom of God and His righteousness, and all these things shall be added unto you.

That means…

The kingdom of heaven is open

God's heart is set upon you

> … God longs to have an encounter with you

And nothing can separate you from the love of God

Your past might not be like that of the virtuous woman in the Bible, but it does not mean God cannot use your past.

We have all sinned and fall short of the Glory of God.

> …And yet many daughters have done virtuously

You are His daughter

You are an heir

You are seated in heavenly places

You are made right with God because of Jesus.

The Bible says if your heart condemns you God is greater than your heart and knows all things.

No matter how you look at life you are known and loved by God

The Story of Bathsheba

2 Samuel chapter 11 introduces us to Bathsheba.

> *2 And it came to pass in an eveningtide, that David arose from off his bed, and walked upon the roof of the king's house: and from the roof he saw a woman washing herself; and the woman was very beautiful to look upon.*

> *3 And David sent and enquired after the woman. And one said, Is not this Bathsheba, the daughter of Eliam, the wife of Uriah the Hittite?*

> *4 And David sent messengers, and took her; and she came in unto him, and he lay with her; for she was purified from her uncleanness: and she returned unto her house.*

> *5 And the woman conceived, and sent and told David, and said, I am with child.*

I love the repeated pattern; notice she is not just known by her name Bathsheba, in this text she is referred to as the woman. Keep in mind Bathsheba was only answering King David's call, when he sent word to her. She must have been nervous and confused, because up to this point, neither of them knew one another and yet she slept with him despite having a husband... now she is committing adultery.

It would seem like this sin should fall on King David alone, after all, because of her beauty he sends for her, uses her, then sends her on her way.

This is relatable to just about any woman alive who at one point or another has been objectified, seen, or touched merely at the will of a man, only to go home wondering what just happened. Not that we are all caught up in adultery, but we live in a culture that objectifies beauty every day, so much so, that we have bought the lie that we are not...

- ♛ Pretty enough
- ♛ Thin enough
- ♛ Young enough
- ♛ Smart enough
- ♛ Worthy enough

No man will want me for who I am...

Bathsheba is a very real woman with very real problems and being with child is one of them. Then there is another problem far more pressing, she must not get caught committing adultery; adultery carried a death sentence being that she was married.

And the moment King David hears about it, he begins to plot this scheme to cover his sin.

> *8 And David said to Uriah, Go down to thy house, and wash thy feet. And Uriah departed out of the king's house, and there followed him a mess of meat from the king.*
>
> *9 But Uriah slept at the door of the king's house with all the servants of his lord, and went not down to his house.*

King David wanted Uriah to sleep with his wife Bathsheba so he could conceal his sin and maintain her virtue while passing the child off as Uriah's, but David's plot fails... But another plot to get Uriah drunk soon follows.

> *[13] And when David had called him, he did eat and drink before him; and he made him drunk: and at even he went out to lie on his bed with the servants of his lord, but went not down to his house.*

Again, the plot fails leaving King David to resort to murder

> *[15] And he wrote in the letter, saying, Set ye Uriah in the forefront of the hottest battle, and retire ye from him, that he may be smitten, and die.*

> *[26] And when the wife of Uriah heard that Uriah her husband was dead, she mourned for her husband.*

Clearly, Bathsheba loved her husband, why mourn if she did not, but soon after her grieving, King David married her. Now the woman is a queen. Though the child fell ill and died, Bathsheba would go on to conceive another child. This child would be called Solomon, King Solomon at that.

The name Solomon means Peace.

Keep in mind King David never intended to marry Bathsheba. He was too busy plotting his way out of the mess he created... a three-fold plot that ultimately made Bathsheba a queen.

God brought peace back into the lives of both Bathsheba and King David after David repented.

God loves, God forgives

God made his peace treaty

While looking at the above scriptures, notice that all the women, despite having a name were at one point noted in text as 'Woman.' It is as if, God was reinforcing the name origin of the first woman, now known as Eve.

God formed you in your mother's belly and called you by name.

God knows your situation. God can turn things around and bring you favor and honor, all while setting you before kings and nations. The question is, do you believe that?

I know what it is like to feel alone, and yet, God's desire is to get us alone.

- ♛ On one hand, loneliness robs us of hope
- ♛ On the other hand, loneliness can introduce you to the God of Hope

Romans 15:13 (KJV) *13 Now the God of hope fill you with all joy and peace in believing, that ye may abound in hope, through the power of the Holy Ghost.*

Still, I have found myself in situations I did not want to pray my way out of...

... any more than I wanted to hear from God.

I felt comfortable in my pain

And running from it made sense.

I thought that the moment I prayed I had to be perfect. I had to hurry up and change. I had to fix. I had to behave. I had to stop sin in its track… I put so much pressure on myself, I did not realize I needed a heart transplant, even though I was already on the donor list… God put me there. He was giving me the heart of Jesus while giving Jesus my busted, clogged arteries, so that He could give me the transplant needed to save my life. And, just like a natural transplant, I would need follow-up care. I would need Jesus to perfect that thing which concerned me…

Keep in mind, when you are on the operating table, you are vulnerable. Everything changes; your blood pressure, your temperature, your oxygen levels and you are put to sleep. You couldn't jump off the operating table if you wanted too, any more than you could hand your doctor a note before the sedation kicked in to tell the doctor how to put a stint into a clogged artery. We cannot tell God how to operate on our heart, no matter how bad the condition of it. Rather than self-medicating, and searching the internet to figure out what is going on with you, look to God, the creator of all living things.

I would strive to be better, but I got worse. I was trying to do heart surgery on myself. I realized I need Jesus!

I sat down with the great Physician and prayed/asked God what is wrong with me and instead of pointing out a life-threatening condition, He gently told me, 'You are in good hands, I have got you, and I know what I am doing.'

Unlike visiting a natural doctor who immediately begins to tell you, "You have to quit smoking, or drinking," God simply said I love you. There were no demands to be perfect because He is the Perfecter through Jesus, the one who died for all.

Suddenly, I realized everything that was wrong about me or in me, was placed upon Jesus. My burden was now His. The death sentence passed down from Genesis 3:15 and John 3:16 had been fulfilled. All I had to do was surrender. Praise God.

I want to point out a few deep things of God that drive this home to our hearts.

The post op for a surgery like this is simple; confess sin, repent, and turn away from sin, and do not touch it. Jesus did the work; transplant complete without incident or complications to the patient.

GOD'S PLAN FOR YOUR LIFE IS BIGGER THAN WHAT THE DEVIL HAS DONE TO IT...

Romans 8

> *31 What shall we then say to these things? If God be for us, who can be against us?*
>
> *32 He that spared not his own Son, but delivered him up for us all, how shall he not with him also freely give us all things?*
>
> *33 Who shall lay any thing to the charge of God's elect? It is God that justifieth.*

34 Who is he that condemneth? It is Christ that died, yea rather, that is risen again, who is even at the right hand of God, who also maketh intercession for us.

...God will freely give you all things together with Christ

- ♛ ...Who shall say anything about you
- ♛ ...You are God's elect (Chosen)
- ♛ ...God Justifies you so you do not have to
- ♛ ...God alone is your judge

...No man can condemn you, they have no right

Romans 8:34 (KJV) *34 Who is he that condemneth? It is Christ that died, yea rather, that is risen again, who is even at the right hand of God, who also maketh intercession for us.*

...Rather than condemn you, Jesus is praying for you.

35 Who shall separate us from the love of Christ? shall tribulation, or distress, or persecution, or famine, or nakedness, or peril, or sword?

36 As it is written, For thy sake we are killed all the day long; we are accounted as sheep for the slaughter.

37 Nay, in all these things we are more than conquerors through him that loved us.

38 For I am persuaded, that neither death, nor life, nor angels, nor principalities, nor powers, nor things present, nor things to come,

³⁹ Nor height, nor depth, nor any other creature, shall be able to separate us from the love of God, which is in Christ Jesus our Lord.

God is for you

Yes, God is for you, and His son, Jesus is for you, and nothing can separate you from the love of God.

Your past can not separate you from Jesus Christ

Your sins can not separate you from Jesus Christ

...Because he is praying for you

It does not matter what people say about you, what matters is what God says about you!

Here is the thing, He that comes to God must believe that he is God, and that He is a rewarder of those who diligently seek him...

- ♚ ...and if your heart condemns you, God is greater than your heart, and knows all things
- ♚ And yet there is a condition to all of this... do you believe that Jesus is the son of God?
  John 3:16 For God so loved the world, that he gave his only begotten Son, that whosoever believeth in him should not perish, but have everlasting life.

1 John chapter 1

> *⁹ If we confess our sins, he is faithful and just to forgive us our sins, and to cleanse us from all unrighteousness.*

The moment you confess that Jesus is Lord, God begins working out His 'Love plan' for your life.

I used to believe that God could save everyone but me. I suppose that is somewhat prideful, and yet I knew my life, not only from my perspective, but from the perspective of others. Others who would not offer me an ounce of forgiveness, never mind the length I had to go to get their approval. Their compassion was about as warm as an icepick.

I had the reputation I could not live down

I committed adultery

I lied, I cheated, I did everything the Word of God warned me not to do...

I did not see a way out. Jesus became a crutch that validated my sin. I used Him, this beautiful embodiment of forgiveness and love to say, "Oh I can continue in sin, Jesus died for me." I regret that...

> [9] *If we confess our sins, he is faithful and just to forgive us our sins, and to cleanse us from all unrighteousness.*

Let me say this, because it is the very scripture that has healed me and set me free from shame and brought truth to the lies spoken to and over me.

He that is forgiven of much,

loveth much

I know that to be true. I walk with God now, not away from him. I remember when I began reading the Bible, I would go out of my way to stay away from the red letters. In other words, I would not read anything Jesus said. Instead, I went to all the smaller books of the Bible and learned of Jesus well before I had an encounter with him through his Word. Now, I find his teachings full of love, rather than condemnation and shame for my disobedience. I love how God moves us through his Word, allowing us to get to know the love of God through Jesus Christ and the comfort of the Holy Spirit.

My heart no longer condemns me, now I cry out, 'Abba,' which is to say Father.

… and when I do not know how to pray, or what to pray because life is hard and people harder, I simply ask the Lord to 'help me'.

The Woman at the Well
A MINUTE WITH GOD IS BETTER THAN A DAY WITHOUT HIM

Jesus has such a tender heart toward women, and women are tender toward Jesus. Oh, how I hope you see the beauty in these encounters...

Jesus said of his ministry, "I can only do that which I see my father doing,"

With that said, keep in mind that when Jesus goes to the well, it is not a coincidence, any more than it is by chance. Jesus was weary, but there is so much to gain from this encounter with a woman of Samaria. Her ill-famed reputation was probably the reason we find her at the well, around noon. Notice in scripture no one else is there, other than Jesus who is literally waiting for her, his entire agenda is set on her.

Sometimes, God will set you up for an encounter with Him, and this (woman) is no different.

John Chapter 4

> [5] Then cometh he to a city of Samaria, which is called Sychar, near to the parcel of ground that Jacob gave to his son Joseph.
>
> [6] Now Jacob's well was there. Jesus therefore, being wearied with his journey, sat thus on the well: and it was about the sixth hour.

The sixth hour which is to say noon, the hottest time of the day. Check this out. It is deep...

Notice scripture says that Jesus was weary...

It also says that he sat on the well...

This encounter is not just an encounter, but a close one at that. After all Jesus could have sat next to the well, or a little far off, but He doesn't. Instead, He literally sits on the well or right next to it depending on which version of the bible you read but according to the KJV text Jesus sat on the well. In other words, He did not just go out of His way to meet her, He made sure He was in Her way.

Jesus is not that thirsty that he should sit on a well, he is after all the well of living water. Jesus will go on to use the well to open a conversation that should not have happened according to customary laws.

> *7 There cometh a woman of Samaria to draw water: Jesus saith unto her, Give me to drink.*
>
> *8 (For his disciples were gone away unto the city to buy meat.)*

In other words, they were busy, distracted, doing something else.

> *9 Then saith the woman of Samaria unto him, How is it that thou, being a Jew, askest drink of me, which am a woman of Samaria? for the Jews have no dealings with the Samaritans.*

As if that were all she was. I have always believed this statement and have said it 1000 times; I listen to what you don't say just as much as I listen to what you do say.

Furthermore, if this encounter was not designed by God, then Jesus would have had his own leather bucket with which to draw water from the well.

And for her to say, "*the Jews have no dealings with the Samaritans*," is like saying, "How dare you ask me for water. Do you not know we have nothing to discuss? Why ask this of me of all people?"

> *10 Jesus answered and said unto her, If thou knewest the gift of God, and who it is that saith to thee, Give me to drink; thou wouldest have asked of him, and he would have given thee living water.*
>
> *11 The woman saith unto him, Sir, thou hast nothing to draw with, and the well is deep: from whence then hast thou that living water?*
>
> *12 Art thou greater than our father Jacob, which gave us the well, and drank thereof himself, and his children, and his cattle?*

Here the woman from Samaria is pointing out what Jesus does not have, as well as, pointing out ancestral ownership, implying with a question, are you greater than he?

> *13 Jesus answered and said unto her, Whosoever drinketh of this water shall thirst again:*

[14] *But whosoever drinketh of the water that I shall give him shall never thirst; but the water that I shall give him shall be in him a well of water springing up into everlasting life.*

Check this out, oh man... so deep!

I love it... **Jesus is sitting on the well because He is the well!**

[15] *The woman saith unto him, Sir, give me this water, that I thirst not, neither come hither to draw.*

[16] *Jesus saith unto her, Go, call thy husband, and come hither.*

[17] *The woman answered and said, I have no husband. Jesus said unto her, Thou hast well said, I have no husband:*

[18] *For thou hast had five husbands; and he whom thou now hast is not thy husband: in that saidst thou truly.*

(Five husbands and this one is not yours implies that he belonged to another.)

[19] *The woman saith unto him, Sir, I perceive that thou art a prophet.*

[20] *Our fathers worshipped in this mountain; and ye say, that in Jerusalem is the place where men ought to worship.*

21 Jesus saith unto her, Woman, believe me, the hour cometh, when ye shall neither in this mountain, nor yet at Jerusalem, worship the Father.

22 Ye worship ye know not what: we know what we worship: for salvation is of the Jews.

23 But the hour cometh, and now is, when the true worshippers shall worship the Father in spirit and in truth: for the Father seeketh such to worship him.

24 God is a Spirit: and they that worship him must worship him in spirit and in truth.

25 The woman saith unto him, I know that Messias cometh, which is called Christ: when he is come, he will tell us all things.

26 Jesus saith unto her, I that speak unto thee am he.

Here the disciples return and marveled that Jesus talked with the woman, but they do not speak up. The woman leaves her waterpot, goes back to the city, and tells the men to come and see a man that told her all that she ever did. This is a great chapter to finish reading; many believe on Jesus after being with him for two days…

But this encounter was designed to be personal. Here is a woman who had five husbands, and now caught with another. Yet God has his heart set upon her. Jesus does not begin the conversation with her reputation. He begins it and demonstrates who He is and what He can do for her.

- ♔ Jesus waited for the woman of Samaria to show up
- ♔ Jesus knew she was on her way
- ♔ Jesus knew the woman at the well
- ♔ And Jesus knows you!

The moment you encounter the King, He crowns you with his love.

It is better to have a minute with God than a day without him.

This is one of my Favorite Prayers,

Ephesians 3

> *[14] For this cause I bow my knees unto the Father of our Lord Jesus Christ, [15] Of whom the whole family in heaven and earth is named,*
>
> *[16] That he would grant you, according to the riches of his glory, to be strengthened with might by his Spirit in the inner man;*
>
> *[17] That Christ may dwell in your hearts by faith; that ye, being rooted and grounded in love,*
>
> *[18] May be able to comprehend with all saints what is the breadth, and length, and depth, and height;*
>
> *[19] And to know the love of Christ, which passeth knowledge, that ye might be filled with all the fulness of God.*

20 Now unto him that is able to do exceeding abundantly above all that we ask or think, according to the power that worketh in us,

21 Unto him be glory in the church by Christ Jesus throughout all ages, world without end. Amen.

God's love is limitless...

God will strengthen you in your inner man

God will reveal his unfailing love to you through Christ

A love that passes your natural minds knowledge

God will do above all that you ask or think...

God works outside of your natural limitations because He has no limitations,

- ♔ There is no end to God
- ♔ There is no end to Jesus the Son of God
- ♔ There is no end to the Holy Spirit

... And despite a natural death, there is no end to you.

GOD LOVED US THEN GOD LOVES US NOW

So far, we have learned:

- ♔ God is merciful toward you
- ♔ God sees you
- ♔ God hears you, and your children
- ♔ God saves you, and your household
    - ♔ God gives you living water/He is giving you himself

The Woman With an Issue of Blood

Two desperate situations happening; one a 12-year-old little girl is dying the other a woman who goes out of her way to get the Lord's attention.

Look at this woman who has an issue of blood found in Luke chapter 8.

Keep in mind Jesus was moving through a crowd. A man named Jairus, a ruler of the synagogue, falls at the feet of Jesus begging him to come into his house and heal his only daughter, 12 years of age, who is dying.

That is deep, considering the woman we are about to meet has had an issue of blood for 12 years. In other words, for as long as this man's daughter has been alive, this woman has been suffering. She'd spent all she had on physicians, and none could heal her. Here we have two desperate situations happening in the presence of Jesus. It is not recorded how long the little girl lay ill, but it is important to note that Jesus knows all things and one of these terrifying scenarios propels Jesus to deal with the most arduous.

In Luke 8:40 the whole story begins.

> *40 And it came to pass, that, when Jesus was returned, the people gladly received him: for they were all waiting for him.*

> *41 And, behold, there came a man named Jairus, and he was a ruler of the synagogue: and he fell down at Jesus' feet, and besought him that he would come into his house:*

42 For he had one only daughter, about twelve years of age, and she lay a dying. But as he went the people thronged him.

43 And a woman having an issue of blood twelve years, which had spent all her living upon physicians, neither could be healed of any,

44 Came behind him, and touched the border of his garment: and immediately her issue of blood stanched.

Stanched is to say, to stop, stand still.

45 And Jesus said, Who touched me? When all denied, Peter and they that were with him said, Master, the multitude throng thee and press thee, and sayest thou, Who touched me?

46 And Jesus said, Somebody hath touched me: for I perceive that virtue is gone out of me.

47 And when the woman saw that she was not hid, she came trembling, and falling down before him, she declared unto him before all the people for what cause she had touched him, and how she was healed immediately.

48 And he said unto her, Daughter, be of good comfort: thy faith hath made thee whole; go in peace.

Note, the woman who was known for the issue of blood for twelve years would forever be known by what Jesus called her — Daughter."

On top of that, according to Jewish belief, a woman with an issue of blood would have been considered unclean and had no virtue. So, when Jesus says, I perceive my virtue has gone out of me, not only does it heal her, it instantly made her clean.

I love the way God weaves love into our life. Not only is He willing to heal you, but God is also willing to accept you into His family...

Let your faith be made known, even if you must do it with fear and trembling. We have a Father in heaven that wants us to reach out and touch Him.

When I began writing this book, I had spent hours talking about faithful men in the Word of God, but I walked away restless. I knew that something was off. My spirit was bothered, not because of the men of God, but because I was still waiting for God to show me something. What he showed me was so profound that I am going to separate it from this paragraph...

- ♚ Throughout the New Testament, the only people that dared to touch Jesus were WOMEN.
- ♚ Yes, a woman touched God throughout scripture.
- ♚ ...Many daughters have done virtuously

It is true men lay hold of Jesus, but that was to crucify him, and Thomas known as doubting Thomas, touched Jesus after his resurrection.

The beauty here is this... while it was common for men to greet one another with a holy kiss, it would have been against the law for a woman to reach out and touch a man; let alone a Rabbi.

Can you imagine the faith these women had? They knew the Messiah, and they touched Him.

- ♟ I want to touch Jesus!
- ♟ Throughout the new testament women literally touched Jesus, something that not even a man dared to do according to scripture.

How beautiful is that!!!!!

I hope, by the grace of God you see it...

One woman touches Jesus.

Another woman anoints Jesus.

Luke Chapter 7

> *36 And one of the Pharisees desired him that he would eat with him. And he went into the Pharisee's house, and sat down to meat.*
>
> *37 And, behold, a woman in the city, which was a sinner, when she knew that Jesus sat at meat in the Pharisee's house, brought an alabaster box of ointment,*
>
> *38 And stood at his feet behind him weeping, and began to wash his feet with tears, and did wipe them with the hairs of her head, and kissed his feet, and anointed them with the ointment.*
>
> *39 Now when the Pharisee which had bidden him saw it, he spake within himself, saying, This man, if he were a*

prophet, would have known who and what manner of woman this is that toucheth him: for she is a sinner.

⁴⁰ And Jesus answering said unto him, Simon, I have somewhat to say unto thee. And he saith, Master, say on.

⁴¹ There was a certain creditor which had two debtors: the one owed five hundred pence, and the other fifty.

⁴² And when they had nothing to pay, he frankly forgave them both. Tell me therefore, which of them will love him most?

⁴³ Simon answered and said, I suppose that he, to whom he forgave most. And he said unto him, Thou hast rightly judged.

I love this part...

⁴⁴ And he turned to the woman, and said unto Simon, Seest thou this woman? I entered into thine house, thou gavest me no water for my feet: but she hath washed my feet with tears, and wiped them with the hairs of her head.

⁴⁵ Thou gavest me no kiss: but this woman since the time I came in hath not ceased to kiss my feet.

⁴⁶ My head with oil thou didst not anoint: but this woman hath anointed my feet with ointment.

47 Wherefore I say unto thee, Her sins, which are many, are forgiven; for she loved much: but to whom little is forgiven, the same loveth little.

48 And he said unto her, Thy sins are forgiven.

49 And they that sat at meat with him began to say within themselves, Who is this that forgiveth sins also?

50 And he said to the woman, Thy faith hath saved thee; go in peace.

Here is the beauty in the way Jesus demonstrates his love...

He knows we are women; and he knows we are sinners!

- ♕ He let this woman touch him with...
- ♕ Her tears
- ♕ Her dirty hair
- ♕ She anointed his feet
- ♕ And her tears and dirty hair cleaned the feet of our King.

... Can you imagine that? it makes me want to cry.

Keep in mind, Jesus says almost the exact same thing to both women...

To one He said, *"thy faith hath made thee whole; go in peace."*

To the other woman he said, *"Thy faith hath saved thee; go in peace."*

Healed thee

      And

        Saved thee

Faith is a critical aspect to salvation, not just for the eternal life we have but every day. I cannot think of one day where I do not need His salvation operating in my life. I wake up and decide daily to choose Jesus. I put my trust in, cling to, and rely on him. There is no other way.

The Woman Caught in the Very Act of Adultery

That feeling you get when your sin finds you out...

John Chapter 8

> *¹ Jesus went unto the mount of Olives.*

> *² And early in the morning he came again into the temple, and all the people came unto him; and he sat down, and taught them.*

> *³ And the scribes and Pharisees brought unto him a woman taken in adultery; and when they had set her in the midst,*

> *⁴ They say unto him, Master, this woman was taken in adultery, in the very act.*

> *⁵ Now Moses in the law commanded us, that such should be stoned: but what sayest thou?*

> *⁶ This they said, tempting him, that they might have to accuse him. But Jesus stooped down, and with his finger wrote on the ground, as though he heard them not.*

I love this, it appears that Jesus is not listening

While they are busy "pointing their finger" at the woman

Jesus uses his finger to write in the sand

> *⁷ So when they continued asking him, he lifted up himself, and said unto them, He that is without sin among you, let him first cast a stone at her.*

> *⁸ And again he stooped down, and wrote on the ground.*

9 And they which heard it, being convicted by their own conscience, went out one by one, beginning at the eldest, even unto the last: and Jesus was left alone, and the woman standing in the midst.

10 When Jesus had lifted up himself, and saw none but the woman, he said unto her, Woman, where are those thine accusers? hath no man condemned thee?

11 She said, No man, Lord. And Jesus said unto her, Neither do I condemn thee: go, and sin no more.

Notice, Jesus is alone with the woman

The encounter begins with a gentle conversation. She had been caught in the very act of adultery, the weight of this carried with it a death sentence and yet...

- ♚ He does not scream at her
- ♚ He does not yell at her
- ♚ He does not condemn her
- ♚ He tells her to go and sin no more...

Jesus is a gentle savior

But He is also a king... and not just any king

He is the Lord of Lords and the King of Kings...

There has never been a time when He was not!

Listen, your life might look messed up in 1000 different ways right now. You might not even like the woman you are today, but that does not mean that God does not love you right where you are... He does love you, always.

Pray for that encounter, that moment, that touch, that look...

Expect Jesus to show up on your behalf, even if you have been caught in the very act!

Whatever that act looks like, it is pale compared to one act of God.

Let your stumbling blocks become stepping-stones...

Give it to God

Confess it, or write it all down, and hand it to the Lord, then burn it...

For we are redeemed by the blood of the lamb and the word of our testimony...

All these women had a story

- ♛ They all had a testimony
- ♛ They all had an encounter
- ♛ They all had the chance to walk away from the lives and lies that afflicted them
- ♛ They all had the opportunity to follow God and touch His son Jesus

Check this parable out. This is one of forty written in the Bible, of those, this one bothered me most...

Until God showed me something so utterly profound, I could not blame God.

I hope you walk away free from shame.

The Parable of the Wise and Foolish Virgins
Matthew 25

¹ Then shall the kingdom of heaven be likened unto ten virgins, which took their lamps, and went forth to meet the bridegroom.

² And five of them were wise, and five were foolish.

³ They that were foolish took their lamps, and took no oil with them:

⁴ But the wise took oil in their vessels with their lamps.

⁵ While the bridegroom tarried, they all slumbered and slept.

⁶ And at midnight there was a cry made, Behold, the bridegroom cometh; go ye out to meet him.

⁷ Then all those virgins arose, and trimmed their lamps.

⁸ And the foolish said unto the wise, Give us of your oil; for our lamps are gone out.

⁹ But the wise answered, saying, Not so; lest there be not enough for us and you: but go ye rather to them that sell, and buy for yourselves.

¹⁰ And while they went to buy, the bridegroom came; and they that were ready went in with him to the marriage: and the door was shut.

¹¹ Afterward came also the other virgins, saying, Lord, Lord, open to us.

12 But he answered and said, Verily I say unto you, I know you not.

13 Watch therefore, for ye know neither the day nor the hour wherein the Son of man cometh.

Here is the beauty,

The bridegroom is coming!

I used to be bothered by the five foolish virgins, until God showed me this...

- ♛ God gave all ten of them lamps
- ♛ Lamps they were to be stewards of
- ♛ But, rather than go to God to get the oil
- ♛ They chose to go to man

You cannot go to man to get what only God can give!

Thy word is a lamp unto my feet, and a light unto my path...

Praise God!

Jesus is the Word of God, the Living Word. He cannot separate himself from it, anymore than you can separate your soul from your body.

The moment you begin to read the Word, you invoke the power of the Living Word to operate in your life. The last thing the devil wants you to know is that the word of God will always reveal the love and grace of God.

Sin Condemns...

Grace sets free

You are God's daughter

You are fearfully and wonderfully made

You are an heir, and a joint heir to the kingdom

The truth is you are seated in heavenly places right now...

God sees you

I cannot stress that enough. Our Father in heaven sees us

- ♕ You see your past
- ♕ God sees your future
- ♕ You see your mistakes
- ♕ God sees your victory
- ♕ You see your dirt
- ♕ God sees His Son

Isaiah 1:18 Come now, and let us reason together, saith the LORD: though your sins be as scarlet, they shall be as white as snow; though they be red like crimson, they shall be as wool.

When you confess your sins, God is faithful and just to forgive you of your sins and cleanse you from all unrighteousness.

Cast your cares upon him he cares for you

God has a standing invitation written in His Word for you

Behold, the Bridegroom is coming

That which has been is now, that which is to be, has already been

There is never a time when you were not...

God said from the foundation of the earth I knew you

I called you by name ... My question is, are you worse than any of these women? I doubt it!

We have all sinned and fall short of the glory of God

Scripture also tells us this about the suffering Jesus went through... Let me expound

> Hebrews 12:2 *Looking unto Jesus the author and finisher of our faith; who for the joy that was set before him endured the cross, despising the shame, and is set down at the right hand of the throne of God.*

You, yes, you were the joy set before him

Before you knew yourself

He knew you

He knew your sins, but he saw you redeemed by the blood of the Lamb

Remember, He that knew no sin became sin for us that we might become the righteousness of God through Christ Jesus

- ♔ He takes our sin
- ♔ And gives us life
- ♔ Eternal life, is eternal love...
- ♔ You are a gift!
  Proverbs 18:22 (KJV) *Whoso findeth a wife findeth a good thing, and obtaineth favour of the LORD.*

Isn't that deep? Most women do not realize they were created to be Gifts!

Everything we do should be done in the interest of the King's crown

You are his daughter and because of that you will be given different crowns

- ♔ The crown of righteousness
- ♔ The crown of life
- ♔ The incorruptible crown
- ♔ The crown of glory

With that comes kingdom protocol...

It is for this reason I bow my knees that the father might be glorified.

Lord, I pray for your daughters

I pray you grant them peace when they feel shame, and that you would reveal your tender heart toward them, that they may see your nail scared hands and the love you have for them, may they see you, hear you as they sit under your counsel Lord I pray you share your heart with them. Make your daughters bold in the profession of their faith and their love walk with you, challenge your daughters Lord to reach out and touch you in the mighty name of Jesus I pray. Amen

Yes, the King of kings and Lord of Lords has a new law

A royal law

A law He himself Completed on the cross

The law of love!

He loves you...

Has crowned you....

Has a kingdom

Has gone to prepare a place for you

That where He is you might be also

You have been called to 'Love one another as Jesus loved you.'

Everything we do in Christ Jesus should be in the interest of His Crown.

Mary Magdalene

In the book of Luke Chapter 8, we meet Mary Magdalene

> *[1] And it came to pass afterward, that he went throughout every city and village, preaching and shewing the glad tidings of the kingdom of God: and the twelve were with him,*

> *[2] And certain women, which had been healed of evil spirits and infirmities, Mary called Magdalene, out of whom went seven devils,*

Mary Magdalene is briefly talked about in this text, but her role in the life of Jesus and His ministry was significant throughout the gospels.

Jesus had an encounter with a woman that most people would have stayed away from. Mary suffered a great and horrifying affliction, to be the host of seven demons. One demon would have been more than enough to trouble her soul, talk about a horror story with a redemptive ending... Jesus cast out seven demons.

Prior to her deliverance, Mary would have been seen, yet ignored at the same time. Can you imagine that? Most women do not feel seen, and yet God sees us. But to be looked upon as a spectacle, as one thrashing around; she would not have been anymore clean on the outside than she was on the inside. Mary would have looked a messy wreck; she was out of it at the very least. Take into account, her demeanor would have been scary, her words violent and threatening, thereby driving everyone away from her. So, the moment Jesus delivers her from seven demons, we see Mary Magdalene in a new light. She is grateful for what the Messiah has done for her,

> ...so grateful that she follows his ministry all the way to the cross, and the grave.

The encounter Jesus had with Mary not only changed her life immediately, but it also changed her drastically... She goes from having a host of demons, to being the first to see the risen Lord. How beautiful is that?

God delivers no matter what afflicts us.

Mary Magdalene followed Jesus to the grave and this is where it gets deeper...

John 20: 11- 17

> [11] *But Mary stood without at the sepulchre weeping: and as she wept, she stooped down, and looked into the sepulchre,*
>
> [12] *And seeth two angels in white sitting, the one at the head, and the other at the feet, where the body of Jesus had lain.*
>
> [13] *And they say unto her, Woman, why weepest thou? She saith unto them, Because they have taken away my Lord, and I know not where they have laid him.*
>
> [14] *And when she had thus said, she turned herself back, and saw Jesus standing, and knew not that it was Jesus.*

15 Jesus saith unto her, Woman, why weepest thou? whom seekest thou? She, supposing him to be the gardener, saith unto him, Sir, if thou have borne him hence, tell me where thou hast laid him, and I will take him away.

16 Jesus saith unto her, Mary. She turned herself, and saith unto him, Rabboni; which is to say, Master.

17 Jesus saith unto her, Touch me not; for I am not yet ascended to my Father: but go to my brethren, and say unto them, I ascend unto my Father, and your Father; and to my God, and your God.

Let me break this down,

Mary knows Jesus was crucified now she is at the sepulchre where they lay him,

Verse 11 Mary stands weeping

Looks into the Sepulchre (the abyss of death)

12 sees two angels who say unto her, Woman, why weepest thou?

In verse 15

Jesus saith unto her, Woman, Why weepest thou? whom seekest thou?

Mary, supposing him to be the gardener…

Okay wait, In the beginning of the word Adam named the woman, woman then God honors Adam's original name. Throughout the bible the Lord refers to the name given unto us in the garden...

Now, Mary perceives Jesus to be the 'Gardener'. Her perception was not off think about this... Jesus is the garden of life, Jesus is the garden of paradise, and Jesus has gone to prepare a place for us.

16 after supposing him to be the Gardener, Jesus gets personal with Mary by calling her by name, Mary.

17 Jesus goes on to tell Mary, "Touch me not,"

Our fall began in the garden of paradise and Jesus's ministry ends the way it began, perceived him to be a gardener but unlike the woman in the garden who said, 'ye shall not eat of the tree, neither shall ye touch it, lest ye die' then touches it

Mary does not touch the Lord, instead she was obedient. How deep is that.

This is the restorative nature of God, where man failed to please God, Jesus was obedient unto death granting us eternal life in paradise.

When God touches our lives, we are no longer the old man, but a new creature in Christ. Mary Magdalene is proof.

ACKNOWLEDGEMENTS

I want to dedicate this book to the Lord, that I may give to Him all that belongs to Him because it is nothing without the Lord.

I would like to thank my mom, Mary Kocol for your diligence in raising us. Mom you are a beautiful woman, both inside and out. You worked hard for this family. I want to honor you because you deserve to be acknowledged. Mom, I wrote this book in honor of God and to bring honor to you. You have been a rock for this family even at your own expense and I see you, I see your love. Thank you for all you have done for me.

I would also like to thank my dad, Norm Kocol who is a deacon in the church. He too is well loved and looked up too. Thank you for pouring into us and not giving up on us when things were less than perfect.

I love you Mom, Dad

Finally, I'd like to dedicate this book to my sister, Loretta Gubin. My best friend, and without you I couldn't have done the things I have accomplished, and Roxanne, my other favorite sister, I am so blessed to be a part of the family and to have beautiful-hearted women who believe in God, and share and fellowship with me. I love you both dearly.

I also dictate this book to all my nieces, you are beautiful. I hope this book shows all of you through the Word of God how truly loved you are, Samantha Hammontree, Jessica Hammontree, Heather Diaz, Audrey Diaz, and Lilly Gubin, you are all in my heart. I love you.

I would like to thank Melissa Vorbeck for being an amazing friend and a safe place to land.

A NOTE FROM THE AUTHOR

It is my desire to see lives changed because of this book. It is the cry of my heart and my hope that lives will change through the power of the Holy Ghost and that your joy is full as you realize we all get dirty on the way home. But God...God can use our dirty hair to clean the feet of a king. You are loved and accepted; now and forever.

Give your heart to Jesus; it's easier than you think. All you have to do is acknowledge you are a sinner, believe that Jesus died on the cross for you, and ask Him to step into your life and make you into a new creature in Christ. He is willing, He is able, and He is waiting. Jesus loves you with an everlasting love; nothing can separate you from the love of God through Christ Jesus.

- A prison sentence cannot separate you from his love.
- A divorce / broken family/ abortion
- A life of depression and oppression
- An abusive husband or wife/ Abusive parents or children
- Sexual assault against you/ unforgiveness
- Drug abuse/ Addictions/Prostitution/ Exotic dancer/Entertainer
- Murder, bitterness, wrath, envy, hate, self-loathing, fornication and adultery, and every other wicked work of the flesh

Yes, these are all works of the flesh, works that God can change, renew, forget, and appeal through the blood of Jesus. I love you, and I don't know you, how much more does your heavenly father love you and He does know you, He knows every strand of hair on your head, has numbered and counted all of them.

Your hair may be dirty, but let God do for you what you cannot do for yourself.

When I look at the above list, the works of the flesh, I see the old me; but I have been redeemed by the blood of the Lamb and the word of my testimony, and I forgive those who have trespassed against me, hoping they too might find the love of God that awaits them.

With that said... I pray with and for you right now in Jesus' name. May God get all the glory as he gives you beauty for ashes, the oil of joy for mourning, and the garment of praise for the spirit of heaviness.

While I hope this book has touched your life, there is a far better book to read, 'The Holy Bible.'

If you asked Jesus into your heart, please feel free to write to me, I would love to read your testimony.

With love,

Paula Hammontree Joseph

ABOUT THE AUTHOR

I grew up on the graffiti lined streets of Detroit, Michigan. I had a hard life but lived harder. In many ways, I live through every character I create. I love writing. It has long been "the great escape" for me.

I am a mess, my hair is dirty, but I love the Lord. If you want to know more about me, feel free to visit:

Paula-Joseph.com

@PaulaMarieJoseph on Instagram

Paula@Paula-Joseph.com

I had a career with one of the largest companies in the United States at the time but found out that I wanted to use every part of my broken past to help others. Before I knew it, I began working on Chene Street in Detroit for an inner-city mission church. I felt complete until I didn't. I fell, and that fall led me into dancing in a 'gentleman's club.' I loved the darkness, the hustle, the compliments, but more importantly, I felt at home. I felt like I belonged to a huge family, one that accepted me, the real me, or so I thought. I still prayed, but church was the furthest thing from my heart. I didn't want to darken the doorstep of another church as long as I lived. I felt like no one made room for me at the cross, and I went with that until I met a woman who spearheaded an organization for women like me.

I met genuine women of God who loved me in spite of my profession.

FOR YOUR REFLECTION

May these pages reflect different aspects and prayers about your relationship with Jesus and the beauty in those encounters...

The God of mercy

The God who sees

The God who hears

The God who saves

The God who restores peace

The God who gives you living water

The God who heals

The God who delivers

The God who forgives

The God who Crowns you with his love

God's loving encounter

God's royal law

The God of mercy

The God who sees

The God who hears

The God who saves

The God who restores peace

The God who gives you living water

The God who heals

The God who delivers

The God who forgives

The God who Crowns you with his love

God's loving encounter

God's royal law

Made in the USA
Columbia, SC
27 September 2021